no secrets.

ja carter-winward

Binary Press 2014

© 2014 JulieAnn Carter-Winward. All Rights Reserved
Published by Binary Press Publications, LLC
ISBN-13: 978-1-61171-025-0
ISBN-10: 1611710251

<u>shh</u>

no,

i'm sorry.

i can't keep a fucking secret.

~jacw

new year

so i decided
that i wanted to make at least
one new year's resolution
that's doable,
so i'm going to start using the word
motherfucker
more often.

cliché

it was a dark and stormy night.
she took off her panties,
the clouds parted,
and he saw the sun.

hole in the asphalt

the hispanic men worked on the road
and gazed up at me as i drove by,
coming down from my big house
on a hill
in my shiny car.
don't they know
when i open my eyes
every day
i gaze into
an abyss
that threatens to
swallow me whole?
i wave at them
as i coast past
their bulldozers
and gloved hands.

artist's hand

my hands have paint on them.
it's an echo of my insides
displayed on every canvas
i touch.
there are so many paintings
because no
one picture
can paint
the inner workings
of my whole self--
so i paint
and i paint
and i paint
and each piece captures
something of it,
some dark corner,
some bright spot,
some undulating line
that makes no sense,
some color that clashes with another…
and then i start over,
while the last piece
i craft
from the inside-out
dries
in the sun.

famine

he made love to me
with a rose
because it was all
he had to offer.

popular

she blew them for fun
then she blew them for money
then she did it
because in their eyes
was the only way
she could see herself
clearly.

care-full

after rough sex
i started to bleed inside.
they had to cut me,
release all of that black and red-
but the cut had to stay open after the procedure
with a cloth drain that had to be pulled out
slowly,
agonizingly,
inch by inch,
 every day
until it healed.
at the time my ex was eager
for me to get back in the fuck-saddle.
sex was so painful
but he didn't care,
which was what got me into trouble in the
first place.
him.
him not caring.

heroes and villains

his impulses are good.
his mother had told him
and he knows she is right.
he listens to
one
while telling the other
it will have its due
when glass buildings topple,
when trains careen from bridges
he will unleash his hero
and save that day-
but until then
he must feed
the hungry beast
who craves
the suffering
of innocents.

eight

i stood at the deli counter
waiting.
it was my sixth stop of the day
and i had two more.
i looked around
and for a brief second,
i bent my knees,
almost going all the way down,
to kneel down on the floor
and sob.

self-amuse

people always seem to look vicious
when they laugh at
their own jokes
made at the expense of others.

texas

our relationship was good by email,
good by phone.
but when i was around him
we didn't click.
i felt like i was in the presence
of a dear friend-
a brother,
but i wanted it to be so much more.
in the end
i realized you can't force something
that looks good on paper
to feel good in person,
no matter how many times
you drunkenly fuck.

woman-speak

women have a secret language
and they speak it through eyes
and the upturn of a mouth,
with hands
and their whole being
rippling in time to unheard music.
their words come out
and they are banal
and harmless;
but that other language they speak
is decibels louder-
i've never understood their language
even though i'm female,
but when i'm around them
i find i understand one phrase:
i've got
we don't like you
down pat.

nostalgia

round-toed keds sneakers again
doll talking to stuffed animal again
grass on my bare feet again
mom's carrot bread again
believing in god again
hot chocolate after school again
our first kiss again
snapdragons magical again
santa drinking eggnog on christmas eve again
grocery shopping fun again
brigham city peaches again
my religion is true again
family badminton games again
my sister a gypsy princess again
paper dolls again
the first boy who liked me again
riding a bike with a basket again
safe when i'm sick again
patches sewn into my pants again
dad's cologne again
feeling immortal again
grandma's backyard tree again
cinnamon rolls on christmas again
easter hymns on sunday again
playing catch with my big brother again
i want it all--
i want it all over again.

estelle

i used to visit her
in her store all of the time.
she is in her mid-seventies
and still bleaches her hair
white-blonde.
she gets body wraps to tighten up
her flabby arms.
i don't come in as much any more
because it's always a chore
to wait for her to ring me up and out.
she's forgetting a lot now.
it could be her age,
but i suspect it's the
vodka on her breath
she tries to hide
with spearmint gum.

why

some people fuck to forget.
some fuck to remember
the everlasting him or her
of that long ago place
when a touch meant
nothing
and everything
and then nothing again.
i remember to forget
the fucking feeling
of feeling
like nothing.

guy

he'd hung himself.
he left behind kids
and two ex-wives
and so someone thought
it would be a good idea
to make a fucking facebook page
commemorating him.
all of his mormon high school friends
wasted no time
putting up
refrigerator magnet sayings
on the page
complete with rainbow graphics,
pictures of kittens
and i thought
what the fuck?
i joined in the fray
and tried to advocate
for his family left-behind,
his kids,
who surely didn't want to hear
banal platitudes about god
and heaven-
this was grief, godammit--
that sinking, black,
hollow, lonely,
angry, helpless,
anguish-place
that has no rapport
with feel-good sentiments
hung up with
this week's grocery list.
i got hammered by them all,
of course-

but the worst hammering came
from the children themselves,
when they said they actually liked
those shallow trite-isms--
and it was then my heart hurt
for my dead friend even more:
his children didn't truly mourn him.
they didn't know him at all.

compliment

it cost me nothing
to tell a ninety-two year old man
he didn't look a day over seventy-seven.

choices

my daughter called me
a fucking bitch
when i had her arrested.
my eyes were fixated
on her bloody wrist
and my stomach
was lurching up
and out of me
but i held firm
and gave her a choice
between juvenile hall
and a hospital.
she was in an in-patient treatment for 13 weeks
and she hated me the whole time.
my job
day in and day out
was to second-guess
everything i had done;
every interaction,
every word,
and sob myself to sleep
each night with worry and regret.
now she's older,
a mother,
and we never talk about those dark days—
but she calls me every day
so we don't have to.

signals

when he moves up behind you,
close--
in the wee hours of the morning.
and you know he's awake,
you know he wants it because
you can feel
it;
and so
you have a choice:
to wiggle your ass in consent,
or pretend you are
fast asleep.

old and new

there's that new love-
the feeling
saturating every thought,
saturating your panties,
glow on cheeks
flushed chest
and you can't get his
cock in fast enough
after panting
and mouths breathing fire...
and then there's the seasoned love-
the feeling
saturating every pore,
saturating your heart
so that it's heavy
and bursting with
contentment
and you can't get his
cock in slow enough
after connecting
and mouths breathing
peace.

old god

when i was young
the notion of god was fostered
not by what they said,
but by the stories.
they told me to call him *father*;
a loving father,
a patient father,
a merciful father-
but he was never a father to me.
he was *god*,
the old god
of the old book
who was vengeful
and petty,
and jealous,
and cruel,
and no matter how many times
i called him
father,
i was always on guard
for that monster
to convene disaster
and visit it upon me
for my   many   many   sins.

the joke

i was
eight,
maybe nine,
and my primary teacher
was teaching us about easter--
she was solemn
as she spoke of the sacrifice of jesus.
not one for tolerating sobriety well...
i asked her
that if god showed his love for the world
by having his son
tortured and killed,
could i do the same thing
using my brother dave?
i was taken to the bishop's office that day
and i learned about the word
blasphemy.

straight a's

the debate coach and i
had an understanding.
he would give me all a's
even though i didn't show up for class.
the deal was,
i would win in the tournaments,
and let him tell me things like
god, you make me horny.

mormon atheist

when i'm in pain,
the worst kind,
i break my vow of silence to
the god i don't believe in
and rail at him
for not being there-
i tell him that if he was really there
he would never allow his children to suffer
the way we all suffer.
it's proof-positive that he isn't there
and i tell him that
and then i remember
no one is listening
to me.

a-name-only

why is it
that in today's culture
parents insist on expressing
their own individuality
through the unfortunate
names they choose
for their children?

bully

there was this new kid in school
and he was bigger and meaner
than everyone else.
he pushed this girl named tiffany
up against the counter once
because he needed a pencil.
i walked up to him and gave him two.
i think he was a bully
because he needed stuff,
like we all need stuff,
and a friend was the one thing
he couldn't get by pushing.
so i just offered,
and he never bothered me.

star-cross

i had a huge crush
on this guy in high school.
he was two years older than me,
with great dimples
and he was in all of the a.p. classes,
which was a prerequisite for any guy
i liked.
i even made friends with his little sister
in the hopes she'd say to me one day,
why don't you come over
to my house after school
today so i can introduce you
to my brother and insist he take you out
and eventually marry you—
surprisingly, she never did.
through the irony and cruelty
of social media
i recently found out
that he might have felt the same way
about me back then.
apparently he was painfully shy
and never had the guts
to ask me out.
it's a shame.
i'm fairly confident that
had he asked me out,
he would've gotten laid.

regret

they'd had a sexless marriage.
then her cancer came back.
it had started in her bones
but it moved to her kidneys,
her pancreas,
and he nursed her
when there was no hope left
for her to live to see
the next grandchild born.
after she was gone
he mourned her
with a fiery,
brutal grief,
a grief that ate away at him
like her cancer
had eaten her.
he was convinced
that had he been able
to make love to her
all of those times
she had said *no*,
she would have lived.
he was convinced
that he would be able to
heal from the loss
if the bed he slept in each night
weren't so full of memories
of a love
he was never allowed to show.

slick

lube:
the lazy man's
foreplay.

dark meat

we separated right before thanksgiving
but we still lived together,
still made thanksgiving dinner
for the kids.
we were so broken
so shattered and tattered--
there was so little left
to weave this illusion together,
but we did it for one day.
during our separation
i fucked someone else
and told him.
i thought he had a right to know
there was no going back,
there was no going forward.
done   done   done.
we played our parts well
until we got to carving the turkey.
he offered me a slab of turkey,
saying,
i know you like the dark meat.
funny thing about dark meat
is that while the size is impressive,
it's not everything
and other skills are involved

if you want to please a woman.
but i never told my soon-to-be-ex that.
let him think
it was the best fuck i'd ever had.
let him think
that fucking someone else
eradicated any hope for us.
let him think it.

<u>dehydrated</u>

he was a man who needed to be touched—
needed arms around him
and hands on him
and legs surrounding him,
needed it like some people
need water
and so when the divorce was final
it had been months
since he'd had that tactile drink.
the couple had come into town and called him
to invite he and his wife to dinner.
but he was not a *them* anymore
he was a *him*
and so they invited him
to their hotel
to explain what had happened
to his *them*.
they had drinks
and soon,
the husband left him alone with his wife
and she took him to the bedroom
and she touched him
with her arms and her hands
and her lips and her cunt

and he drank her in--
big, ravenous gulps
as if he had climbed,
belly first,
into an oasis
from the arid sand.
he knew that very few people would understand.
he saw that night
as a sublime act of kindness
where others would find scandal
or perversion.
but the real perversion
lies in beds
all over the world
where people thirst,
night after night,
sometimes alone,
sometimes inches from someone,
without that simple comfort
he was offered
by another man's wife.

sign

i seem to have a sign
on my forehead that clearly reads,
dear strangers who like to
over-share your personal
lives;
please, please
talk to me in
the fucking elevator.
I want to rip my head off every
fucking time.

a little bird

i began scandalizing my mormon ward
early on.
i was disfellowshipped
more times than i could count—
that means i couldn't ingest the bread and water
(the body and blood of jesus)
in church
and once the job of taking roll
in my class
was suspended
because of
my scandalous behavior.
my mother bore the brunt of it
because she was a woman
and all of the women in my ward
were talking
talking
they were always talking,
and my mother bore the shame
of having such a scandalous daughter.
i want to send every woman
in my former ward
my books
and say,
you can stop talking now.

fait de compli

there are days
when naming five types of apples
is my greatest accomplishment.

equanimity

she got his credit card
and he got to say he was dating
a stripper.
it was as clean a transaction
as any lap dance.

annuals

on my birthday
my husband was very affectionate
and it was clear he wanted to take me back to bed
that morning.
i reminded him that i wasn't a man,
didn't need a yearly blowjob,
i wanted him to fuck me every day anyway,
and if he really wanted
to make the day special,
he should just make me breakfast.

resembling the remark

invariably
when in a group of people,
someone brings up
another someone
(who isn't there)
and begins to recount tales
of that person's lunacy.
is something wrong with him?
someone asks.
is he bipolar?
someone else asks.
and the answer is,
invariably,
probably
or maybe even tri-polar-
much to the delight
of the crowd.
i fail to see
how someone's suffering
is continually a source of judgment
and laughter.
i want to join in, so i say:
maybe he has multiple sclerosis, the asshole!
all heads turn toward me.
it seems that a painful, chronic illness
suffered somewhere besides
the brain
lacks comedic effect.
then i leave
before someone says something else
too ignorant to ignore.
see, i have an illness to manage

and i don't want to be the topic of conversation
the next time
i'm not there.

precipitation

i wonder if the earth feels
cleansed after a good rain,
like humans do after a good cry.
i wonder if it takes in
shuddering thunder-breaths
and feels tired and empty,
numb as the tears glisten on the leaves
and roads—
if the sun feels too bright
but the warmth feels good
on its face,
and then it feels ready
to face another moment
 in eternity.

<u>need</u>

the big term in pop-psychology
in the 90's was
co-dependent.
everybody is co-dependent.
i am, you are,
they are
all
co-dependent.
the gurus preached that it was
unhealthy to *need* anyone.
all you need is yourself.
so i guess i am.
i'm fucking co-dependent.
i need my family.
i need my partner.
i need the people i love,
and i'd like to see those gurus
back in the paleolithic days
telling a tribe
they are too co-dependent
on each other.
i'd like to watch the tribe
eat them.

alive

my lover offered
to accompany me
to my mother's funeral.
this was odd to me
because lover
is adult-speak for
fuck buddy,
and fuck buddies don't come to
your mother's funeral
where they meet your children,
your siblings,
you aunts
your in-laws.
it was the first indication
that maybe he was more.
after the funeral
we went back to my house
and we did what we did best.
but this time
unlike any other fuck buddy moment,
i cried.
he fucked me
and i fucked him
and amid all of that pleasure
was this pain and this refrain
that
my mother is gone
my mother is gone
and then pleasure again.
i knew from the outside looking in
that fucking like that
was strange.
but on a deep level,
the level where grief rests,

it seemed like the most natural thing
i had ever done.
i was alive.
we were alive.
and my grief would have eaten me whole
had i not had the comfort of his lips
his hands,
his cock.
it felt like something
terribly important was happening
and i was honoring
the old gods--
the old gods of
fuck and death.

meaning

dreams are supposed to be symbolic.
there are people who make a living
interpreting dreams,
so i'd like to hear
their take on the one i had last night.
the world is populated by a bunch of zombies,
but the zombies are still
sentient;
they are still our husbands, our sisters,
our friends....
the only way to keep them from eating you
was to be diligent about wearing a certain lotion
all over your body.
the only way to kill them
was with root beer.
okay all you dream interpreters...
go.

sweets

going down on a woman
is like a box of chocolates.
you can't stop
once you've started,
even if you want to.

rebound

i started dating karsten
after matt,
which wasn't very cool
since they were friends.
but i'd always liked karsten—
he didn't have the frat-boy mentality
of matt's other friends.
karsten owned his own home,
he cooked,
he drank gin and tonics.
he was a grown up.
he was the responsible one
in a house full of former frat brats
who couldn't quite put their college days
behind them.
karsten was hard to crack—
always smiling
but something deep inside him
fooled us all
and we couldn't ever get to it.
it was tough
getting him to fuck me.
part of me wondered if he'd been gay

because he didn't act like
a ravenous man
hungry for sex
when i was clearly ravenous
all on my own.
he fucked me sweetly,
gently
and decidedly
un-ravenously.
i think he might have loved me though,
because one night
he admitted to me
that he did coke
and sold a little on the side.
there weren't many people
he told.
he was respectable, after all.
there was so much about him i
didn't understand—
he was unknowable.
after he told me about the coke
i had to re-think everything.
i had two daughters.
cocaine was a big deal.
i finally made the call—
i told karsten
i couldn't see him anymore.
his lifestyle was a risk
i didn't want to take.
three weeks later
karsten killed himself.
i don't think it had
anything to do with me.

let us prey

the stages of grief
never go away.
they shift,
they pass,
they come back with a vengeance
on holidays
or anniversaries,
and the most insidious stage
is bargaining.
which is why
mormon missionaries
are so successful
with people who have suffered a loss.
they promise you that you will see
your mother again,
your beloved nana,
your child;
you can be sealed to your loving husband
for time and all eternity.
they profess to be a bargaining chip,
an instant salve that will take you
out of your grief and
turn it into
a fucking fairy tale.
i can see the allure—
there were times
when i would have sold my soul
to see my mom and dad
again—
a family forever.
then an angry pit grows inside
as i think of all of those vulnerable people
listening to those naïve,
earnest,

ignorant 18- year old boys
telling them
they get a free pass-card
from experiencing
what it is to be human.

shh

no,
i'm sorry.
i can't keep a fucking secret.

abandonment

my aunt called me
because i was the only one
she could call.
my mother
didn't want the boys to know.
my aunt had found her with the pills
in her hand.
i called the hospital
after telling my mother
she had to go.
she had to go.
i checked her in alone.
they went through her bags
as if a 70-year old suicidal woman
had some fucking contraband.
it's dehumanizing enough--
but they strip you
of the last of your dignity
by taking your laces.
then they told me i had to leave.
she sat on the tiny hospital bed
with her default-setting smile on her face
and i could barely talk to her,
could barely breathe for how badly i hurt,
how much i just wanted to take her home,
take her back
to the days when she could do everything,
be everything,
mothering six of us
with sure hands
and smiling eyes.
but they told me i had to leave
and she looked so slight, so frail
on that hospital-issue bed

with its starchy sheets
and standard blue-weave blanket.
everything about her was smaller,
and i had to reassure her that this was where
she should be,
when where i wanted her to be
was twenty years ago,
singing in the kitchen
as she made us sunday dinner.

breath of life

he could literally make
my heart stop.
but then
he got it going again
with his special brand
of south to mouth
resuscitation.

amore

there are songs,
stories,
poems
and art all devoted
to the explanation of love.
i think they all miss certain
relevant points.
for instance,
love is relishing
those bits
that dangle over a toilet
and devouring them
with your mouth.
love is not getting gaggy
when your partner is
puking up their guts
in the bathroom.
changing an adult diaper.
popping that white head on his back.
watching her have a meltdown
during pms
while she shrieks like a banshee
that she hates your mother and she
hates you.
it's kissing in the morning
and thinking
his morning breath is actually okay.
love is committing,
every day,
to the *every day*,
knowing that one day it will end
and the object of your love
will be hooked up to a machine
or covered in blood

and you are willing to invest everything
until that moment
when they leave this earth,
promising them
that if you can help it,
they won't have to do it alone.

choke hold

as i sat in my car waiting
for my husband to run into a store,
an older couple came out together
to their car,
which was right next to mine.
they were in their fifties,
maybe early sixties
and he was opening her door for her.
she turned to him, smiling
and then he did the most curious thing:
he brought his hand up to her throat
and clasped the front of her neck
as if to choke her--
he held his hand there,
all the while
smiling a small smile and
gazing into her eyes.
she smiled back at him and placed
her hand over his wrist.
i watched them
and the strangeness of his gesture
suddenly seemed
like the most natural thing.
he held her life in his hands
with this reverence,
and she let him
all the while
moving in close
for a tender kiss.

perfume

i knew he was right for me
the first time he spent the night.
he had fucked me the night before,
once in the middle of the night,
and then in the morning,
that lazy
from-the-spooning-position fuck
when my eyes hadn't fully opened
and the heat from his body
mingled with the heat
under the blankets
so that it was all this delicious warmth
wrapped around my limbs—
it was after he left
when i knew.
i went back to bed
and as soon as i lifted the sheets
the perfume
of our fucking
wafted up
and it was like nothing i'd ever smelled before;
it wasn't me
and it wasn't him,
it was *us*,
and i got back into bed
and jacked off,
the sheets over my head
that smell curling into
my nostrils
smelling like something
exotic,
and yet smelling,
for the first time,
like home.

empty

i feel extremely sorry
for anyone who is handicapped.
i know it must be incredibly difficult.
but i would like to ask them all to please
get off of their asses
and do something out and about
or please—
let me park
in their fucking spaces
which are always,
invariably
empty.

betrayed

she was my mother's best friend.
she had the voice of an angel
only matched
by the deep resonance
of my father's baritone.
they often sang duets together
while my mother played
the accompaniment.
they sang in the
mormon tabernacle choir together.
we were all in the same ward.
one day they were rehearsing a song
for a church roadshow,
a love song
from a popular musical,
and my mother happened to look up
into the mirror
gracing the piano's upper shelf.
she saw the way her friend and my father
looked at each other,
and it was at that moment
my mother knew.

road rage

the weather was inclement
and the suv was riding my tail
even though i was going faster
than the cars in the right lane.
i pulled ahead a couple of cars
and moved over so he could pass.
before he could,
a slower car moved in front of him
so that he was stuck behind two slow-moving cars
in both lanes.
i laughed out loud
and marveled at how deliriously happy
that made me.
then i thought to myself,
holy shit, i'm an asshole.

the blame

he was bipolar
and he would swing like a pendulum
between self-medication
and extreme religiosity.
but what was ever-present,
always,
was the shame.
he was convinced
that satan
bedeviled him
to drink
and even through his alcohol-soaked breath
he pontificated
on the goodness of god,
the truth of mormonism,
and the weakness of his character.
i wanted to shake him
and tell him that his god had forsaken him,
and so had his devil.
i wanted to tell him
that he held the answer
right in his hand,
if only he would reach out with it
and clasp the rope of reality.

ability

she got injured
and used it to get what she wanted.
then she used it to get out
of everything else.

other people

you think other people will show up
so you don't.
but the others don't
either.

selfish

the brain plays these
marvelous tricks, you see.
the distortions,
contortions,
abortions
of everything worthwhile...
and everyone would be better off
because i am a poison,
a burden
with nothing to offer
but pain.
and these are the tricks their minds play
and it happens too much.
i have lost too many people
to this type of death.
then others, misplacing their anger,
declare
that they were
selfish.
but
if they could have seen and felt
the pain
they would never make this
misguided verdict.

if only
the emotionally and mentally tormented
could bleed
on the outside--
if only the doctors would
provide the morphine
that would barely touch the agony...
then no one would call them selfish.
they would say things like
i don't blame them
and
bless their hearts.
but we can't see that kind of suffering.
we can't see
their exposed nerves
and the will to live
slipping from them
like a wet glass
from the hands of a drunken
soldier.
but maybe if we did see the blood
we'd know.
and someone would be able
to reach them in time
before
their tricky minds
beg them
to do something...
anything...
to find peace.

fences

back in the day,
fences were short.
fences had 3-inch spaces between the slats.
women would come out
with their baskets of laundry
and they'd come just as the morning sun
geared up
for the afternoon heat.
they would talk
and gossip
and sometimes the gossip was for nothing
and sometimes it was
everything--
the sharing of information
that ended in a family in crisis
receiving a much-needed meal
or a neighbor
checking in
on someone alone.
the laundry would catch the sunlight,
trapping it inside its fibers
and the cloth would wave
like friendly hands
in a breeze.
today's fences are vinyl
with no spaces-
today's fences are twelve feet high.
if they aren't enough
we plant the poplar trees
like sentries
guarding our private property
and no one knows
whose mother passed
or whose child has

pneumonia.
we take our private lives
and carefully craft them
into what we want the world to see;
we delete the unflattering picture,
we un-friend those who say
what we don't want to hear
and those we do let see us
never really know
what we look like.
our privacy is complete,
our facades complete,
and no one can ever see
our laundry,
our stains.
we are alone in our suffering
and our fences
keep the world
from hearing
our screams.

i am

i am addicted to caffeine and nicotine
and probably sex.
i am addicted to exercise
but only the good-feelings part-
the hard work part i sometimes skip,
foregoing the good-feelings.
so that technically might not be an addiction.
i'm not addicted to food (anymore)
and i'm not addicted to chocolate,
which i think should only be a garnish.
i'm addicted to writing
and reading.
to sum up,
i could give them all up
except
the sex, exercise, writing and reading.
but that's almost all of them so i guess
i might as well stick with
the caffeine and nicotine, too.

fucking with fuck

why does religion
fuck
with our fucking?
what does fucking have to do
with god?
if god created stuff that feels good,
why wouldn't this deity
want you to do it?
it's like me making
thanksgiving dinner
and then telling my family
they're only allowed
to eat the beans.
and if you eat the other shit.
you have to clean out my garage.
i think of all of these pubescent boys
walking around
aching inside,
a war going on between
what they are—a product of biology,
and who they are told to be.
like religion takes this knife
to your very being
and slices with fear
and shame
into your fabric.
there is so much
to fight against
in this world of ours,
it seems insane to accept
that from the moment we turn twelve,
we have to take that fight
into our own being.

halloween store

and then you get outside
and all you can smell is the
chlorine,
the woman with wild eyes
says to me
as i walk in.
she passes me by
still talking-
chlorine,
she says.
the floor is black
the ceiling and walls are black
with color sandwiched between them
like an open gash.
a couple shops for costumes
that conveys how *together* they are
you see?
cowboy and sexy indian,
cop and sexy convict
she is mine
and i am hers.
the overweight woman
tries on platform heels
for her goth costume
as fake fog plays a backdrop
for a boy
with a plastic sword.
chucky is real
shrieks the four year old girl
as she runs to her mother in line.
her older brother
no more than eight
staggers toward her
with the rubber mask askew on his head.

the father demands,
do you want to be chucky or freddy?
freddy, he says
but not before menacing his toddler sister
who screams
in the cart.
put it back then,
says the father.
the boy chooses to be the molester of children
who slashes them in their sleep.
the music plays aural horror
as i ask for colored hair spray.
orange, i say
i need orange.
i can't breathe with all the black
and color
in between
with the chucky
and children
and so much fake blood.
i get out of the store
and i hear a small voice-
lady,
lady,
you forgot your keys.
the boy hands them to me
and i thank him as he walks away,
freddy's bloody claw still on his hand.

branding

she stopped going to
the mormon church a while ago.
instead
she goes to another
christian church
because their brand of crazy
was much more palatable.

black and white

mistakes.
we all make them.
so when my daughter's friend
from high school
had the department store call me
and ask me if i was her mother,
i lied and said *yes*.
she was almost graduated, had a scholarship.
she was under so much pressure
and she did something she had never done before.
she shoplifted.
i pretended to be her mother
and told them
it would never happen again
and they didn't press charges.
she didn't get a record,
and she went on to do
the most amazing things with her life.
i don't regret one thing i did that day.
it's not often
we get to make mistakes

and learn from them
without them fucking us up
in some real way down the line.
i was glad i gave her
that chance.
i think it saved her
from much bigger fuck-ups
down the road.
i'm always in awe
of the shades of gray
presented to us
in a world where black and white
dominates morality.

bait n' switch

i knew a woman who got married
and they were swingers.
mostly threesomes because she was bi.
so her husband got to help her fuck
other women,
watch her fuck other women
and he got to fuck other women
sometimes, too.
then about ten years in
she told him she wasn't bi anymore,
that it was a misguided personality quirk
brought on by the need to please men.
so it all stopped.
i think for him that would be the same feeling as
a woman marrying a really
successful doctor
and then one day him telling her
they were going to sell
all of their stuff and home
and move to a small town in
south america
to open a free clinic.
i bet it felt just like that.

anthole

there's this guy who calls himself
an artist
because he pours molten metal
down an ant hill,
lets it cool,
washes off the dirt
and *wah-lah!*
art.
seems to me the ants had a lot more to do
with creating that art than he did,
and they would get some of the proceeds
of his sales
if it weren't for the fact
that they're all fucking dead.

melting

when i made a snowman as a kid
i'd always use charcoals for his face,
a real wool scarf
and a big long carrot for his nose.
my dog would always jump up and get
the carrot
so she could gnaw on it
in the corner of the yard.
then the sun would come
and beat down on his head
creating these rimy craters
that would cause his charcoal briquette-eyes
to sink into his skull.
his stick arms would droop and fall
to the ground,
and soon, his body would slump to the side
like it was under some sort of
terrific weight.
i think about all of the yards
with decomposing,
gray-ish snowmen
and how
they belie
what happens
to the families
inside the homes--
cracking apart,
sinking,
returning into the ground
so that they are
one day,
unrecognizable,
even to those who built them.

fucking festive

as i age
i can't refer to the holidays as anything
but *fucking festive*.
the taste is bitter on my tongue.
it's all so sugar-coated--
this good-will
jesus-comsumerism-santa-light-a-fucking
candle-have-some-fucking-egg-nog-buy
a-fucking-trinket-for-your-nail-lady
bullshit.
and it pisses me off.
because for all of the
homogenized, pasturized,
apple-electronic-sized merriment
there are people,
everywhere,
suffering.
they only see
the empty place at their table.
they only note
with this detached wonder
that they don't get to go to their mother's
christmas buffet anymore,
they only see a single tree
in a single life,
no one to share it with
and no one to hold
when the temperature drops
and the lights with their lambent hue
cast a shadow
on the absent,
the missing,
the mourned.
there is sadness and suffering

in too many people
for me to buy into the merriment
of christmas
without an ache inside
for the christmas
they don't sell you
on t.v.

old friends

i saw someone i used to work with
back in my twenties.
she lives in my town
but we worked together in wyoming
for a summer.
she thinks she's a big deal
because she owns 3 restaurants with her
husband.
our eyes met
and she quickly turned away.
now every time i see her
i have to laugh at the
acrobatics she engages in
to avoid me.
i want to reassure her,
tell her i don't give a shit if she talks to me.
i also want to tell her i never liked her much--
so we're good.

pc

there's this big controversy.
should you say *merry christmas*
or *happy holidays*?
from where i sit
it really doesn't matter
when you don't have
any fucking money.

whitewash

my ex-husband
was (said my lawyer)
a terrible parent at best
and an abusive prick at worst.
the custody battle took 2 years
and over 50 thousand dollars.
my daughter ran away from his house at 14
and didn't speak to him for four years
because he refused to meet her demand:
go into therapy with her.
she has since reconciled with him,
and i'm glad for that—
but
it's funny how time can erode
memory
like an old, rusted car.
he still hates me for everything.
i never saw him hurt them—
i only took their word for it
because when a child
is having her soul stripped away
she has to tell someone.
it's my job, then,
to remain the devil in his eyes.
but i imagine one day
my daughter will have
the courage to say to him
dad, it was me who told her about you.
it was me.

open poem to winter drivers

maybe you think those pink fuzzy dice
hanging from your rear-view mirror
or your stripper mud flaps
have secret powers;
maybe it's that painted-on 4x4
lettering on the side of your truck.
maybe it's the tires that are a foot taller than you—
maybe all of that makes you think you can
drive like that in the winter.
but none of those things
will protect you from icy roads
so how 'bout you slow down,
you selfish, ignorant fuck.

wayne

he is imposing,
a big man
and if he looked at you
the wrong way
it could turn you
cold inside.
but that wasn't wayne.
he was sensitive
and easily bruised at times,
and his daunting stature
menaced his own feelings
as much as anyone else's.
he had been in the war
wanted to fight the good fight
and crashed into the desert in '91

with the american flag
at his back
and the patriotic dogma
still wet on his lips—
and he saw too many things;
things he can't talk about
without vomiting in the library
when he decided to find out
why he had been told
that his service was honorable.
and no one could blame him
for his intentions
because nobody knew back then,
even him.
now he writes poetry
to make sure he's still real
and can't watch the news
without flinching,
and when anyone tells him
thank you for your service,
he dies a little
inside.

thought experiment

here's how it works:
go outside
on a rainy day
and think positive thoughts.
tell the rain to stop
and the sun to shine.
remember,
you create your own reality.
let's see how that works for ya.

perfect pitch

when he showed up,
the party at my house
was in full swing.
his presence electrified me anyway,
but i wasn't prepared for him
pinning me in the hallway
and chomping down on my neck.
i was especially not prepared
to have a screaming orgasm
in front of ten of my friends
and my sister.
i didn't know my neck could do that.
i didn't know my sister
was in the room.
the next day she left me a note that read:
i didn't know you could reach a high "c".

connect

i don't mind talking to people.
especially if we've been shoved together on a plane
or in a long line at honey baked ham.
funny thing is,
i never get thrown together
with chatty people.
chatty people are always in the seat across from me
or behind me.
and they hit it off—
like,
they're fucking bff's
by the time we land.
so in line at honey baked i see
a chatty cathy two people ahead of me
making friends with the guy ahead of her.
the guy in front of me is captain silence
and the lady in back of me
is *trailer-hitch betty*
so i don't even want to fucking talk to her
but then i realize that's my problem:
i'm too damn picky.
so i make eye contact with *captain silence*
and say something like
what a line, huh?
he just nods at me
and turns back around to face front
and so i pronounce him an asshole.

mil

i'm pretty sure
my sons-in-law
think i am
the coolest mother-in-law
ever.
that,
or the scariest.

the music

i was seeing this bass player
and he introduced me
to his band,
but all i remember was meeting
mindi.
she was the lead singer
and had this contralto voice
that felt like dry silk
between your thighs.
she was fucking the lead guitarist
but she was married to some guy
from the middle east.
this guy was rich as all fuck—
i mean yacht-and-private-plane rich.
he was back in his country while she was here,
singing.
i saw her changing one day
and she had these full, pendulous breasts
and stretch marks on her hips.
i found out she'd had a couple of kids
with her husband

and she'd dumped them off at her mother's
who lived in town.
she'd sing a song called
sugar
and it was sweet
and dark
like liquid chocolate
going down your throat.
to me
she was this exotic creature--
and sometimes i wonder what ever happened to her;
i wonder if she finally had to face the music
with that husband of hers.

unicorn

bi-sexual women.
my experience is as follows:
there are the young ones
who need to drink too much
and when they reach that particular
level of buzz
after their third appletini
they grab their girlfriends,
drag them out on the dance floor
and proceed to undulate
all over each other
and kiss
with an enormous amount of tongue
as soon as five or more men
crowd around them to ogle.
there are some who take a lot less
alcohol,

but need their male beloved
gazing on them to perform.
these are the serious ones
that will actually get naked and
go down on each other--
but if you get them alone,
without their audience
they feel
weird.
the ones who are less *lipstick* are like this-
they can take or leave the booze
and definitely don't need a man watching
but get pissed when you don't call after
because they want to get some crocs and a couple of dogs
and set up house.
therefore i submit
that there are no truly bi-sexual women out there
except me.
all i want is
female recreational sex.
i don't need booze,
an audience
and i don't want to meet
your fucking mother.

cum

in my twenties
i pretended it was okay
to shoot it in my hair
and on my face.
in my thirties
i pretended to like the taste.
when i got older,
i just started to spit it out.
don't get me wrong—
i still like sucking cock
but--
i like it as more of an appetizer
rather than
my meal.

omd

i remember
listening to
orchestral maneuvers in the dark,
this 80's band,
the first time
i showered with a man.
i remember being in the shower
looking down at his cock
and thinking
oh my god
i'm naked
in the shower
with a guy.
holyfuckinggod
that was cool.

stuck

i was seventeen--
my mother was pounding
on the bathroom door....
what was i doing in there?
i told her i was sick.
what i was really doing?
sitting with my legs open
on the bathroom rug
trying with everything i had
to pull out
a cum-saturated sponge
stuck inside me.
there was no way
i could tell her
and i just remember wishing
i could fit my whole
goddamned fist in there.

time

don't you dare
fucking tell me
you don't have time.
that's what a long-time friend
wrote to me
in an email
in response to me asking her
if i'd pissed her off.
i don't have time, she said.
you moved, she said.
i'm so busy, she said.
i'm a firm believer that you make time
when you want to make time.
so don't fucking tell me you don't have it.
say i'm not worth it,
say we don't have anything in common anymore,
say i'm boring or fucked in the head
or difficult or exasperating
but please,
don't tell me you don't have time for me.
it insults us both.

timeline

birth—don't remember;
childhood—confusing;
i write.
early teens—what's wrong with me?
i write.
mid-teens—something's wrong with me;
i write.
late teens—everything's wrong with me;
i write.
twenties—babies, divorce;
late twenties—drowning in sins;
thirties—re-marriage to escape sins;
i write.
early thirties—last baby;
late thirties—divorce;
write. write. write.
forties—final marriage, true love;
write.
mid-forties—confusing, what's wrong with me?
something's wrong with me
everything's wrong with me
write about sins--
true love.

bygones

my love is ferocious.
my loyalty is ferocious.
my care is ferocious.
if you can't handle
this type of ferocity,
then get the fuck out of my way.

size

a lot of women say
size doesn't matter.
i guess i can see
what they mean on some level.
see,
some men have huge cocks but they
forget that their tongues
and fingers
are just as important as their cocks.
men with little cocks get that.
but then
there's anal.
when it comes to anal,
size matters a lot.

i'll show you mine

my poetry
is like my own
personal
speculum.
you can either handle
looking inside me,
or   you   can't.

d.j.

he was always overweight--
ever since i knew him
and the next quick fix
was always
the fast track
to losing.
last year
it was minerals.
we didn't cook our food
over fire anymore
so we're lacking
those fat-melting minerals.
and the government was in on it.
on what?
everything.
and arguing with him
was pointless
because you're either *one of us*
or one of them.
and disproving the conspiracy
only proved to him
just how deep
the conspiracy went.
they wouldn't let him fly
helicopters
because of his weight
and i saw how angry he was at the world
and what a comfort it must be to him
to believe
that everything was simply
out of his control.

friendship

all of my closest friends
are men.
i think it's because
women find me threatening—
i'm too straight forward and honest.
that, and my potty mouth.

the devil

we met at a party
after months of
talking each other in and out
of bed online.
i wasn't sure i wanted him
in that way;
but i wanted the part of him
that thumbed his nose at
being politically correct
and reveled in being
a horny male—
that dangerous part he showed me
tantalizingly tinged
with sensitivity.
i kissed him on the couch
and i think he called me
a little slut
when i grabbed his hand
and shoved it at my crotch.
and he was right
because when he asked
if i wanted to get a room

i didn't hesitate.
he got me in the room
and then he took me;
took me
in the way those pathetic
girl-porn novels
depict that make all of those
bored housewives
cream their sweatpants
and fantasize
while their husbands watch sports.
yeah,
he took me.
and then i had to go home
to children in their beds
and a husband relegated to the couch
for the past six months.
i was sure
every one of them could see—
could see it right on my face.
i would never be the same;
i had been completely,
unequivocally
hijacked
by a devil.

us

youth forgives.
i never understood
why people use pictures of themselves
when they're young
in their obituaries.
we are not ourselves in our twenties
or even our thirties or forties.
the lines on the side of our mouths
and our eyes
tell how much we laughed;
the creases in our foreheads
reveal our worry;
the callouses on our hands
reveal our work
and play;
the shine in our eyes
tells of our love for life
and our compassion for others.
the weight in our bellies
belies all that we hold dear
and who we have succored.
youth is a pallid reflection
of who we are meant to be,
and our grace
is revealed to the world
in the imperfections
we carry
until we meet our end.

curious

i didn't stop to wonder
what the hotel desk clerk thought
when the woman i was with and i
asked to get a room
at 10 o'clock on a
saturday night
with no luggage.

debate

i suffer from self-doubt.
i wonder what's wrong with me
and the friendly part of my brain says
nothing.
and then the more sinister part of my brain says
everything.
and then a distraction comes along
and the debate recedes
for an instant--
and then i start all over again
when everything is still.

it's not you

we'd been dating 6 months
 and he had gone out of town for work.
when he got home,
i was beyond relieved.
i'd called him one night and he didn't pick up
and i had wondered in a jealous panic
where he could be
at 9 o'clock at night
in a strange city.
i decided to come clean when he got home,
told him
how insecure i'd felt
when he didn't answer.
his eyes changed
and he got defensive
and...
i don't remember the exact wording
of it,
but he let me know
in no uncertain terms
that we were in
very different places
when it came to us.

tissue

i feel closest to my husband
when he uses his cock
to dry my tears.

4/3

my parents died
on the same day,
one year apart.
april 3rd...
the spring,
when days are bright and chilly
or gray and wet;
the day was bright when we buried my father,
wet and gray for my mother.
some people might think that there is some
spiritual connection
as to why they died on the same day.
if there is any truth to that,
then my theory is
they knew we would mourn them
on the anniversary
and they wanted to make it simple
for us.
they had made everything else
so fucking hard
that perhaps this was a final kindness,
a final way to say
we did our best.
i'm pretty sure it had nothing to do
with each other.
a year wasn't nearly long enough
for them to be apart.

truth

we give a lot of lip-service to honesty.
honesty is a virtue—
that is, until someone is being
dishonest
in front of others
and you know the truth.
then there is nothing you can say,
nothing you can do
in a socially acceptable way
to make it honest again;
and the feeling inside you is sickly
and dark
because the person doing the lying
has hijacked your integrity
and made you a part of their deception--
you are forced into silence
while they betray themselves.

resolute

i suppose i'm cynical
as well as judgmental.
i wanted to go to the gym—
hadn't been in a while,
not because i'd not worked out,
but because i work out at home
and at a private gym with a trainer.
the gym was so crowded
there were no parking spaces,
let alone treadmills.
of course, i thought,

it's the second week of january.
see, this is the time
when everyone decides
to change their lives.
all they need is that number to go
from 2013 to 2014;
all they need is for it to be monday.
all they need
is to wait until after
the office party,
the holiday,
the birthday,
the super bowl.
these are the people
who disappear
by march from the gym,
so i can go back and run
on the treadmill in peace.
true change
isn't a fucking new year,
day,
event, or a
round number.
when you are ready to change
you do it--
you don't wait;
and every day you make a choice
to continue the path you've selected
because every
single
fucking
day
is a new day,
a new year,
a new event,
a moment of truth,

a gift.
so you can take all of your
new year's resolutions
and shove them up your ass.
if you wanted to do it,
you would have done it already.

godsisters

having female friends
is a lot like being in
the mob.
nine times out of ten
when they are all smiling
to your face,
someone is behind you
ready to launch a fucking bullet
into the back of your skull.

shamed

i think we all have
moments in our past
that make us feel ashamed.
i have a few.
quite a few.
but the moments that shame me
the most
are the times
i got behind the wheel
when i was shit-faced.
i think of how many ways,
and for how many people
that could have gone wrong.
like i was invincible.
like i knew more than
the statistics.
i was selfish
and naïve
and stupid.
i get pissed at myself
just thinking about it.

na'wlins

i had a woman
pronounce me a slut
in new orleans.
she was commenting
on how many beads i had
around my neck.
i couldn't argue with her--
i'd earned them proper.

therapy

the bishop in our ward
ordered us into therapy.
the therapist's name was stewart—
he had this nose like a giant,
veiny strawberry--
bulbous,
and fat, loose lips.
his voice was really nasally
and he listened
as i told him how i had been dragged up the stairs
by my hair,
held by my neck to the wall.
he asked me then if my husband ever
tripped me or flicked me with his finger.
before i could answer, he asked:
tell me
*what did you **say** to him before he did those things?*
and something inside of me snapped.
i stood up
and leaned over the desk

until my face was inches away from his,
and i said,
i don't know, stewart;
what would i have to say to you
to make you hit me?
we never did go back to therapy.
but the therapist reported our session
to the bishop,
pronouncing me
a very disturbed young woman.

used up

i remember the first time
in my adult life
when i could afford new clothes.
i had always bought used,
even for my kids.
they got one new pair of shoes, one new
pair of pants
and a new shirt for the first day of school.
and i bought them at
wal-mart.
the rest of their clothes were all used and
hand-me-downs, if i was lucky enough
to score them.
so when i finally bought a brand-new shirt
from a small boutique in my new town
i felt giddy
and lucky
(and ashamed)
and self-indulgent
(and wasteful)
and i felt bitter
and humiliated
that i was never able to give my kids
the opportunity
to feel those things.

verboden

when i finally started high school
my mother forbade me to date
one particular guy.
see...
he was the son of her
big boss
at work.
you see where this is going
don't you?
i mean
what choice did i have?
i guess
when he broke my heart
that was the payback
for me being
incorrigible.

american family

when i first got married
my step-daughters didn't like me.
one made it a point to tell me
her *mother* didn't like me.
i'd never met the woman,
so i'm not sure how she could
make that call.
one day the step-daughter told me
her mom said
your dad married someone with small boobs.
i found that funny,
since the ex had gotten a bad boob job
and consequently,
her small boobs
were transformed into big, uneven boobs.
i told my step-daughter that
my self-esteem was sufficient enough
that i didn't need a boob job
to feel good about myself.
i hope she passed that along.

origins

from the time i was old enough
to find boys interesting
i had a huge crush
on my brother-in-law's
younger brother.
it was my first sense of sexual taboo
because he was
sort of
related to me.
it shaped the way my sexual
boundaries worked forever, i think--
or
my sexual boundaries were fucked up
from
      the
           get-go.

owl's talons

the artistic temperament
has been romanticized
again and again
but no one knows what it means.
capricious, indelicate, rambunctious,
solitary, misanthropic, unsociable—
i always took it to mean
suffering.
i don't know an artist
who doesn't suffer
on some level
either for his art,
because of his art,
or despite his art.
the death toll is immense;
death by rope,
death by shot gun, or the most maudlin,
death by oven
as the children sleep
nestled in their beds.
i read the words penned
by the suffering
and i restrain myself
from idealizing their pain.
and from my own suffering i know this:
their creations emerged
in spite of their anguish,
not because of it.

god is

the problem with believers is,
they fail to see the virtue
in the profane.

the change

i remember in my youth
thinking that i would be spared.
my mother went through
what they call
the change
and it was mildly amusing
to see her open the windows
when it was 30 degrees out.
women who get hot flashes
all say the same thing:
they fan their faces and say
whooo!
so when i started getting them at night
i thought about when i was young
and how i never considered
that it could happen to me.
maybe i was in denial.
allow me to help you,
all you young girls reading this:
it's going to happen to you,
bitch.
you're not immune,
so get real and get ready.
there.
feel better?
i do.
whooo!

pretend

i played barbies from the time
i was in kindergarten.
i played with a few neighborhood girls
but they eventually grew out of them.
i didn't
for way too long.
later one of them told me
she didn't like how i played
because i made the dolls do
nasty things.
i guess i never did
grow out of that.

inappropriate

my mother
endowed my siblings and me
with two things uniformly:
a bionic sense of smell
(it's my super power)
and the gift of inappropriate laughter.
nowhere was safe:
church, school, funerals, quiet meetings...
if we all attended together
and one of us caught the eye of another,
it was over.
my sister attended my daughter's choir
performance one year--
my daughter was to perform a duet.
we sat in the jr. high stadium together
and we both noticed someone

had too much perfume on.
we recognized it (cheap)
but couldn't place it--
our super olfactories were being
assaulted.
about 10 minutes into the performance,
i realized the origin of the scent;
the woman in back of me,
her knees about the same level as
my ears,
was the offender.
but i realized it wasn't perfume at all,
but the fragrance of
vagisil vaginal cream
wafting from between her legs.
when i realized it,
i was just barely able to eke out the information
into my sister's ear
before we both just *lost* it.
people were telling us to
shhhhshh....
but man,
we were so out of control
we were *crying*.

personally

i am a fool
for tap dancing,
irish dancing and clogging.
i love them with all my heart.
fun fact.

ashamed

i walked out to my car
and i saw a large woman,
the kind with an oval, flat ass
loading her car.
i kept looking—
i don't know why,
but when she turned to look at me
i saw--
she had a half of a twinkie
sticking out of her mouth
while she used both hands
to load her car.
and i wish i hadn't seen it.
i wish to fucking god i hadn't seen it
because her eyes looked to me
for understanding,
and mingled with that
was panic,
and pain,
and shame,
and i looked away,
continued to my car
but i wanted to tell her
it was alright,
that she was alright;
i wanted to tell her,
but
her mouth was full
and for some weird reason
my eyes were, too.

too

i am too much.
i am too opinionated,
too flamboyant,
too honest,
too political,
too sexual,
too unabashed,
too talkative,
too blunt,
too much.
this too
has a strange, polarizing effect
on people.
they either love me from the
moment they meet me,
or they dislike me
with a fiery passion.
i can never win anyone over,
but i consistently
turn people off.
the problem is
for all of my desires to *fit in*,
i lack the desire to
conform
in order to fit in.
it's a conundrum
i'm still learning to live with
every day.
but of course,
i also think
too much.

back pain

we had plans,
it was a saturday night.
we went in to a little
hole-in-the-wall
sushi joint.
the hostess seated us
and i watched her walk away
and it was only then
i noticed
her protruding belly.
she was probably six,
maybe seven months along.
she walked
with her hand on the small
of her back,
clearly in pain.
i felt so shitty,
watching her working
a saturday night,
her body working over time
to nourish and protect
that baby.
i wondered how many days
that hole-in-the-wall place
would give her
after that baby was out.
and suddenly
i just couldn't think about it
anymore.

mine

sometimes mine is creamy.
it's mostly wet,
but it's been known to
dry out.
sometimes it's sharp,
razor sharp--
it can cut.
sometimes it's
soft,
swollen,
bloody,
inveterate.
sometimes it feels like
it can go all night,
never stopping.
sometimes it smells too strong,
sometimes it's sweet.
it can ruin a person's day
or make it.
it can be all-consuming
or quiet and hidden away.
that's mine.
your turn:
what can your tongue do?

executor

i checked with them,
and they agreed.
see,
i'm married to a man

who is not much of an animal person.
that being said,
i have three cats.
if i die,
what will happen to them?
so i made the decision to
verbalize my wishes,
which is legally valid.
*you are to keep them
alive until they die,*
i said.
my husband agreed.
*bring them up from the basement
every morning on time.
wet food in the morning,
dry food at night.
vases will get tipped
and hairballs will appear
on your pillow if this is not done.*
agreed, he said.
*and you must love them,
you must cuddle them,
stroke them,
talk to them.*
he promised me he would.
*they will leave grumpies
in the shower if you ignore them.*
he understood.
then i asked the cats
if this was acceptable,
and they all *meowed* in assent.
and then my husband pronounced me insane.

coming out

i sang my first solo
at the age of two.
with childhood and early adolescence,
there came the awkwardness
with performing,
so i didn't sing again until
i was fourteen.
i had an idea in my head that i could sing
because i'd sing along with
olivia newton-john on the radio
and it sounded okay.
a girl at school played the piano for me
and taught me a song
called
you're not alone.
it's a song about god
always being there.
i performed it at a talent show
at church,
much to the surprise of just about everyone—
i could sing!
i still remember
every word of that song,
and i still wish
more than anything
that i wasn't alone.

slam

i decided to accept an invitation
to compete in a slam poetry competition.
my poetry was so different
from everyone else's
(not to mention i was 20+ years older
than everyone else.)
it seems if you're not
trans-sexual,
a rape survivor,
gay,
possess families with at least
one suicide,
or had been molested,
you really have no way to win
in the slam poetry world.
the order of the day
was whoever had the biggest pity party,
the most cheesy, hallmark-moment endings
got the highest scores.
i only got to the second round,
then i went over time.
but i was pretty sure
my poems
wouldn't win
because they don't
yank at the heart-strings.
i don't aspire to that;
i never have.
i simply want to
punch you
right in your fucking guts.

the whisky

i knew i had to go while i spent the summer
in l.a.
even though i was only sixteen.
i was seeing a guy
who was twenty-one
so they let me in.
he tried so hard to look cool,
my date.
he had aryan blond hair
close-cropped
because he was just off
a mormon mission.
he'd bought me southern comfort
and let me drink it in the car on the way
just to let me know
how cool he was.
you know,
how
california mormons
are different than
utah mormons...
so by the time we got there
i was too fucked up to remember
who was playing.
i always thought it was
black flag.
it could have been another favorite band,
x.
to this day i don't fucking know.
all i remember
is that blond fucking date of mine
standing out
like a target,
and me just waiting

for some skinhead
to fuck up his shit.

torture

we all torture ourselves
to some degree.
one of mine
is a slip of cardboard
with the words
estee lauder on it.
i sprayed it
once
with my mother's perfume
at a department store.
i saw it today
and picked it up
without thinking,
breathing in deep.
and it was torture.

beauty

i don't believe in beauty
that can be washed away
with a baby wipe.
i don't believe in beauty
that originates
in a surgical room.
i don't believe in beauty that is
sprayed on,
glued on,
or invasively sucked.
i don't believe in beauty
done with the airbrush
and computer programs.
i don't believe in beauty
from the outside-in.
beauty is honest,
authentic,
and paradoxically
imperfect.

new year redux

so i had this dream
that i was making a porn movie
with henry rollins.
that part was very cool.
the part that was weird was
that there were muppets everywhere.
just to be clear,
we were not having sex with muppets—
they were just all around us
with their muppet-hard-on's,
some furry, some different colors,
all pretty impressive.
the point is,
i decided that my new
new year's resolution
was to use the phrase
muppet-fucker more.
and henry…
call me.

update

i am no longer
addicted
to caffeine.
please
make a note.

social media

i have to be polite
on my social media sites.
this goes against my nature
but it's worth it to avoid
the unpleasant drama of
social media conflicts.
the secret to saying
whatever the fuck you want to say
is to find a cute little
graphic that says it for you.
then all is forgiven.

queen

apparently
the word *cunt*
is the queen mother of all
curse words
in britain.
so when this books gets sold
over there,
i want to be known
as
queen mother cunt...
get those pesky bugs
outta their asses.

stable

i have an old boyfriend
who is my friend on facebook.
he dumped me--
not the other way around,
which was statistically
unusual.
whenever he comments
on my posts,
i get this stupid petty thrill
and i seriously wonder
about my stability.

under where

we were watching
salem's lot
but what we were really doing
under the blanket
could keep him
from going on a mission.
i remember because
it was the first time;
he slid a finger
into my cunt.
i thought the pleasure
would kill me.
what it really did
was make him break up with me
so he could safely go
to brazil.

anal

there are two kinds of people
in this world:
those who don't care
when all of their stuff
slides to the floor
from the passenger seat
when they stop short,
and those who will risk life and limb
to retrieve it all
while still driving.

monster

i had a monster hiding
under my head
in every relationship.
i figured it came from my mother.
she told me
about my dad's affairs
when i was just in jr. high.
and the monster rooted itself deep inside.
i was afraid i was just like him,
and in turn,
that every man i loved
was like him, too.
my solution was to meet
the monster head-on,
on its own turf.
as an adult
my lover and i got on adult websites,
went to adult parties,

met with couples.
i figured,
if it was going to happen
i might as well have some
control over how, when and where,
and with whom.
it never happened.
he never met anyone,
and i never met anyone,
and the reason is that
people in that *lifestyle*
were not looking to
enhance anything in their relationships.
they were looking to
circumnavigate it.
we were just looking
to create an experience
that would heal me.
when he didn't find anyone else,
even with my permission,
it did wonders for me.
i decided to stop looking
for ways to heal with other people
so we could find ways
to heal me together.

wrench

there was a lady next door
at my apartment complex
named linda.
she was in her late fifties
and had grandkids,
so when i asked her to watch my kids for me
i told them her name
was grandma linda.
linda had agoraphobia—
she could barely go outside
to take out the trash.
she smoked
and loved the way i sang.
she was good to my girls
but when i think of her
a wrench twists in my gut.
i left them there
to go out;
dates,
parties,
bars,
i was looking for something
in those days
and it wasn't found
staying at home
and being a good mother.
it was an escape
from the clamor
in my head.
but that's no excuse.
i can't go back
and have those moments again
because my daughters are all grown.
i want to tell every single mother

with clamor in her head
to stay home,
savor it,
but they won't hear me,
they can't.
and so they will have their own wrench
to deal with--
metallic,
heavy,
and irredeemable.

heart

i see him
walking.
walking…
we have huge hills near our house
and he wears his earmuffs in the cold.
he is over seventy,
thin as a rail,
trudging up and down those hills
and it's morning,
it's evening
it's afternoons.
i can't drive in or out of the neighborhood
without seeing him
walking…
a neighbor told me he had been a smoker
and had had a heart attack.
the doctor told him
to quit smoking
and start moving.
and so he never stops.
it makes me wonder
how close he had come
to tasting the finality of death—
what had he seen,
where had he gone
to drive him to walk
seemingly all day long
on our undulating streets?
i wonder if,
as he walks,
he feels death
treading behind him,
waiting for him to slow to a halt.

masochism

my name is j.a.
and i have a problem:
i am a masochist.
but i can't help it;
writing is my life.

alone

i can spend time on the computer,
emailing,
chatting
or on social media,
but the only time
i don't feel utterly
and completely alone
is when i finally retire to the sofa
and curl up
with a good book.

state of mind

every man in a relationship
has a box living in his mind called
danger;
it's in a room called
things she doesn't need to know;
it's in a house called
keeping the peace—
in a town called
sexuality,
in a city called
guilt,
in a state called
justification,
in a country called
wisdom.

family values

she didn't believe in
the mormon church--
she's not sure she ever did,
even though she got baptized,
and married a returned missionary
in their temple.
her husband didn't believe either.
they didn't like
the closed-mindedness,
the guilt,
the shame,
the judgmental nature of it,
the clique-ish members,
the cognitive dissonance with
the mythology.
yet,
he was the elder's quorum leader
and she was in the young women's
presidency
and they went to church every sunday.
i asked her why,
and she answered
we go for the kids.

rep

i didn't date much in high school.
none of the good boys took me out
because i had a
rep.
the bad boys only took me out
once
because they found out
pretty quickly that
the rep was a lie.
all i really wanted
was a boyfriend.

self-assess

most of us
undervalue,
and overvalue,
the wrong things
in ourselves.

the matter

this poem
has been floating
in my consciousness
for days.
i haven't been able to speak it,

write it,
or acknowledge it
because of the feelings
it evokes in me.
it was a few years back,
and i went to an event sponsored
by my home ward/church that
i grew up in.
i showed up,
a shiny new adult,
and saw a guy i'd grown up with.
we'd had a rocky,
sometimes hostile relationship
throughout jr. high and high school
and weren't close,
but time forgives the small slights
so i approached him.
he was talking to a man
currently in the ward—a therapist,
someone my parents were fond of.
he was also a former professor
of mine from college.
i walked up to them to say
hello,
and i stood,
and stood,
and stood,
and waited…
but neither of them
would acknowledge me.
      at all.
after a few minutes,
i walked away
feeling diminished,
ashamed,
shunned,

and spurned.
i try to examine why
this affected me so profoundly.
i try to see
what buttons those men pushed
inside of me
to cause me to feel so small--
so bad, in fact
that writing it out
brings heat to my face
and a leaden sensation in my chest.
i'm going back
to another ward event tomorrow—
i was invited,
and my only trepidation
is seeing those two men again.
i think it was the fact
that i was treated like
i didn't matter.
and maybe i don't,
not to them.
then again,
maybe i matter to them a whole fucking lot
and that's why they made such an effort
to shut me out.
i want them to not matter to me.
i want to close a fucking door
right in their fucking faces.
unlike the last time,
when i naively thought i could be friendly,
i'll be prepared.
tomorrow,
i'll matter to them in
a whole, different way.
and then they won't matter
at all.

stranger

there is nothing easy
about a divorce
no matter what
the attorney ads say.
there's the buildup—
no divorce is sudden business.
the final decision might
be precipitated by one thing,
but the buildup?
no--
that
is a process,
whether the couple is
aware of it
or not.
then when the heat dies down
there is a coldness,
a darkness;
this cold front
is the front for
pragmatism.
his stuff,
her stuff,
their stuff.
division,
percentages,
and if applicable,
the multiplication factor:
children.
there is the rallying of allies;
family,
friends,
and the assignment of blame.
there is that nervous pit

sinking inside your gut
and you can't eat
but you're secretly glad you're losing weight
because the dating market
is tough enough
without the added weight
of *actual* weight
to contend with.
you lose a whole side of a family
and don't know
who to trust.
everything shuts down
and a large portion of your brain
is in this black hole
while you're working
or talking to someone about
anything other
than the break up.
but the hardest part,
the part that really burns inside,
is when you suddenly see
a person you thought you knew
change into someone
completely different.
and then you're left to wonder
why you hadn't seen that person
all along.

the dark

there is a buzz of excitement
in these parts
as the cold, dry winter
starts to abate,
and dead, yellow ochre grass
peeks through the grimy,
crusty snow.
people start wearing shorts
while it's still 60 degrees,
as if somehow their will alone
makes it warm enough
for summer clothes.
the days get longer
and the winter blah's start to lift—
but not for everyone.
not for me.
i dread spring and summer
like most people dread the cold.
and i feel it coming.
it's coming like a dark blanket,
readying to smother
the breath right out of me.

couple

i was a blogger,
once upon a time—
well-known in the
ex-mormon community.
i came to the blogger party
with another well-known blogger
only he went by a moniker
on his blog.
when we got there i introduced him
and there was a large hum
of excitement from the crowd.
you two are together?
one woman asked.
i affirmed that we were.
she looked at us and said,
i'm going to go home
and masturbate to both of you.

henry and anais

he was henry miller;
he broke it off
with me one night
because he needed to date another woman—
someone from his past.
then he said that
i was his anais.
i told him
henry miller never stopped loving anais;
so he ought to have known
right then
that i was the one
he should keep.

thunderous

we were in the bar
finishing off the last of our pints
when a huge thunderstorm hit.
we went outside
and stood in the rain next to his truck.
i knelt down and gave him head
while lightening lit up
the sky,
and the thunder clapped,
sounding like applause.

dis-labled

my brother is a doctor
of physical therapy.
his job is to hurt people.
if he doesn't hurt people,
he's not doing his job.
you wanna walk again?
get the fuck out of the chair
and move.
you wanna use your right arm again?
quit your whining
and pick up the dumbbell.
here is a phrase you will not hear
in his office:
oh, it's hard? well then, let's not do it.
so why is cognitive therapy different?
therapists get to listen to people
complain about their lives,
and some people make therapy
a career,
or a hobby,
like fishing,
like golf.
they come with the same dilemmas
every week
and there isn't a therapist alive
who will say,
get off your ass and walk
three times a week for 30 minutes
and you can stop complaining
about the size of your ass to me.
no, they nod, say
i hear you're struggling with your self-image;
what would you like to do about that?
the answer?

they won't do a fucking thing.
the only way they get better
is to kick their own ass.
and most people in therapy
don't want to be uncomfortable.
i say we cross-train physical therapists
to be cognitive therapists.
we'd see a sharp decline
in our victim-centric culture
where everyone walks around
saying
poor fucking me.

remember

when i think of my mother
her hair isn't gray.
it's brown
like it was all my life,
except that weird stint
when i was two
when she went platinum blonde.
when i think of her,
she remembers who i am,
and she listens to me and
gives me advice
even when i don't want it.
mostly
when i have a problem,
she would just say,
i'm sorry
and
i love you.

when i think of my mother
she is wearing her running shoes still,
because she'd just run 5 miles.
she's cleaning
and something is baking
in the oven.
she's talking in a silly voice,
or singing with her vibrato
out of control.
she isn't taking thirteen pills
that i had to get from the pharmacy,
cut and organize in her weekly pill box;
she isn't looking at me
with a vague smile
and sad eyes.
if i think about my mother
in her last months,
weeks or days,
i feel awful
because i feel relieved
that she is out of her pain
and i don't need to care for her,
worry for her,
anymore.
so i think of her with her brown hair
and then
the incredible sadness i feel
makes sense.

jack n' steve-o

we'd make out under the houseboat
and he would feel me up
under my lifejacket.
he was going to be a senior—
but not just any senior,
a student-body-officer-senior.
in my neck of the woods
s.b.o.=popular=mormon (usually)=
rich parents,
which was obvious since it was his parent's
houseboat we were under.
i was naïve and just wanted him
to like me.
it was exciting
that he was all of those things.
i dreamt of the homecoming dance
coming up that fall.
at night he'd situate his sleeping bag
next to mine atop the houseboat.
i'd want to hold hands and kiss more.
too risky.
one night he took my hand
and wrapped it around his hard
little pencil cock
and had me jack him off.
this is what people don't get about sluts:
we don't want the sex,
servicing sexual needs doesn't get us off.
we want to be liked,
and with mormon sluts,
we didn't know how to say
no.
the male was our ticket
to everywhere we wanted to go.

in my case,
homecoming,
popularity,
belonging,
meeting the cool kids.
when high school started,
he talked.
my reputation was ruined
before homecoming even arrived.
he did not ask me
to the dance.

timing

when someone says
i got married too fast,
i think they're understating
the problem.
i can't see how an extra 6 months
of dating,
a few more walks on a beach
or living with someone
is going to make that person more suitable
for marriage.
no—
when they say that,
what they really mean is,
i made a big fucking mistake.

tattle

we were friendly over email,
flirty over chat
and naughty over text.
his wife found out
and threatened to tell
my husband.
i didn't have the heart to tell her
my husband already knew.

use

when i was useful to her
she wouldn't leave me alone.
now that i'm not,
she's gone.

saved

she had a baby in her
from a one-night stand.
she wouldn't talk to me about it
because she was on her way
              out
as my friend.
but our mutual friend told me.
she started doing a lot of drugs
before the abortion.
after,
she kept on with the drugs,
thinking they would save her.
looking back
i think the baby could have saved her
because now
she's just a fucking
train wreck.

holy cow

i met him at this bar called
the holy cow.
he was a rising musician,
had a hit single on the radio.
we danced after his show
and he asked me up to his room.
i declined.
#thingsiregret.

accommodations

my lover brought up the champagne.
he left us alone in the hotel room
and closed the door behind him
when he left.

gender-bender

they say i write like a man,
like that's supposed to be
the ultimate fucking compliment.
i say i write like a woman
who isn't afraid.

glass

i have a histrionic cunt.
anything other than flesh in it
and it goes all out of balance and i need
pills or a cream to get
all the cunty flora and fauna back on track.
then,
going through my drawers,
i found a glass dildo
i'd forgotten about.
thank god.
we're back in business.

closet

there's a guy i know
running for congress.
i think he should fuck me.
every politician needs
some kind of skeleton
in his closet
to keep him humble.

re-collective

i love to talk to people
who knew my parents;
we reminisce and share anecdotes
and they seem closer,
as if our collective memory
somehow brings them
back
to
life.

oil and water

divorcing someone
who has difficult personality traits
for you
will not solve the problem
if you had children.
one or more of them
will develop those same traits
and you'll have to learn to deal with
them anyway--
only this time,
in a place of acceptance.

impotence

the political realm
is a place we're not allowed
to visit
at family parties.
everyone gets too riled.
this should also be a social media rule,
but it isn't.
i guess
we the people
need to be able to say how
disenfranchised,
disillusioned
and helpless we feel
as politicians
in local and national
government
continue to stick it in our asses.

directions

the most painful memory i have
of being a parent
is how often i had to parent my children
from the horizontal position.

patience

if you come and read what
i'm writing
over my shoulder
before it's finished,
i will cut you,
motherfucker.

tear-jerk

what does it say about our society
that we need theme music
and a scripted video
about veterans returning home
for us to give a shit
about what the fuck is going on?

never

there's a tag line from an old 70's movie
that reads,
*love means never having to say
you're sorry.*
what the hell?
love means
always having to say you're sorry
because we are always doing
stupid shit to hurt other people.
always.

mister-understood

the way i fight aging
comes in different forms.
i'm angry i have this brain now,
this self *now*,
instead of 20 years ago;
what a fucking waste.
my anger honed in on a target,
and i didn't see it for
what it was.
i was indignant,
and indignation
is always a justifiable.
i was scathingly judgmental
of older men
who seemed obsessed
by younger women.
i called them
emotionally stunted

when i was being kind,
and *pigs*
when i wasn't.
i was irrationally angry at them.
i felt rejected--
angry that i was no longer the object of desire,
rejected as a whole population—
our selves,
our experience,
our sagging tits,
our laugh lines,
our gray roots.
so i judged these men
as they pined for the
suppleness of youth.
but i didn't see
that men fight aging, too.
they are terrified
of that spare tire,
that receding hairline,
the sudden and inexplicable waning
of desire
that used to motivate their days
and nights
in a constant, walking
boner.
i still don't pretend to understand.
but i stopped being angry,
i stopped feeling rejected—
they are searching for something;
they are afraid, too.

factory

there is no tongue
as razor-sharp
as an insecure snob's.

process

i hate it when people
ask me about my
process.
whether it's writing
or painting—
it sounds so fucking
pretentious.
okay, here's my process:
i sit down and write shit
from my guts.
i slap color on a canvas
until it looks right.
that's my fucking process.
clear it up any?

abreast

there isn't a woman alive
who isn't aware of her cleavage.
she may act nonchalant
when it's hanging out,
but she knows its power.
make no mistake.

intentions

sometimes my darkness
oozes out onto other people.
i try to tell them
to stay out of the fucking way.
they insist
they can see a light.
but really,
they're just seeing
the illumination
from their own
expectations.

irony

the car ahead of me
had a bumper sticker that
proudly read
i buy local only.
the car was
japanese.
the driver was white.

men and women

would you sleep with her?
 would i? no. but I could.
you could?
 yeah, but i wouldn't.
but you could. what if i said you could?
 then i could.
would you?
 then i would.
if you could.
 right.
you're an asshole.
 what did i say?

defining moment

when i asked her if she and
her boyfriend had had oral sex,
she said yes.
i asked her if she knew
what oral sex was.
kissing with tongues,
she said.
with the cunning use of my
hands as puppets,
i showed her
the correct definition.
her eyes were saucers.

limitless

someone told me once that
because i didn't like sports,
i was limiting myself.
to what
i asked…
to…
art, books, poetry, children
family, films, travel,
photography,
and sex?
yeah.
i'm really missing out.
enjoy that kick-off.
i'm going to go have
an orgasm.

the station

i worked at a shop
that specialized in lactation.
they sold everything breastfeeding,
including pumps.
we had *try-out* rooms
where lactating women could go
get milked by battery or electric
powered pumps.
that was the worst part of it for me:
cleaning breast milk out.
it made me gag.
the owner and her husband
were nice to me—i was just
divorced with two kids
and needed a job.
the owner was a bigger woman,
pregnant,
and still had a kid on her teat
who was four years old
(gah)
and a few more at home.
one night as i vacuumed,
she was counting out the register
and the husband watched me vacuum.
he asked me if i worked out.
apparently my tight pants
and snug shirt gave me away.
the owner scowled at him,
then at me.
the next day i got fired
for being 10 minutes late
back from lunch.

on writing

there are times when the words
blaze
because they came so fast.
there are times when they
sit and cure
like a painting.
then you're done.
and then you want to
put it in the hands
of anyone and everyone
who has that look
in their eyes that says,
i feel so alone.

poetry

it isn't poetry unless it rhymes.
it isn't poetry unless it has meter.
it isn't poetry unless it has
f
o
r
m.
it isn't poetry.
this
isn't poetry.
like a big blue canvas
isn't art.
like jackson pollock isn't
an artist.
like *house of leaves*
isn't a novel.
like travolta
isn't an
ac-tor,
like bukowski isn't
a poet.
like seeing a cheetah hunt
isn't beauty.
like clean water is without
micro-organisms.
like shittily isn't an adverb.
like the pure,
unadulterated meaning
of all things
can be defined
by the small-minded.

banned

her mother was the bishop's wife and
she didn't like me
but she tolerated me
playing with her daughter.
she thought i was
a
bad influence.
snooping around in her mother's
books
i found a novel called
wifey
by judy blume.
my friend let me sneak it out
and when i read it
i learned all
i needed to know
about sex
at the age
of ten.
i think it's safe to say
the bishop's wife
was a very good influence
on me.

class

i'm consistently amazed
at the pride some people have
in being low-class
and ignorant.
it seems to suggest to them
a sort of
salt-of-the-earth
ordinariness,
handed down to them
generationally
that reveals a level of integrity.
i don't have the heart to tell them,
*no, it just means you have no class
and you're ignorant.*

grope

you want an instant lesson
in the difference between men
and women?
try grabbing a woman
suddenly
between the legs.
the reaction
would not be the same
as a man's.

the father

i don't think god and jesus
talk to each other.
jesus spoke about compassion,
about easing the suffering of others,
of helping those in pain
and not judging.
it occurred to me
that all of those lessons he taught
might not have been for us
but instead
were for his dad.

a dream

there was a time
when penmanship mattered.
when a high school diploma meant
you could spell,
construct a proper sentence
and do basic math.
there was a time when that diploma
had clout
and you could walk into a job interview
and have a shot
at something with
upward mobility.
you could feed your family on that job,
and even save money and buy a home
with a fence.
there was a time when hard work
meant job security

and you'd make shift manager one day,
then manager.
your pay would increase
and you could afford another car.
there was a time when
an average bag of groceries
was ten dollars,
and it cost less than twenty
to *fillerup*.
that time was before my time.
things started changing
when i was a teen
and they kept changing
so much so that
the *american dream*
is now just
the *american memory*.
even though it was a long time ago,
i remember it.
i remember it like it's hard-wired into me,
like an imprint on my insides.
it resides in there
like this residual hope
that somehow
we can resurrect the dream
and anoint it with a new purpose,
we can call it forth
like a miracle
and celebrate the life
we were meant to live.

piece of mind

hey god….
about today;
fuck you.

winnow

i was going through
all of my facebook friends,
deleting people i don't know,
people with whom i never interact.
some people i want to delete but can't;
it seems like such a hostile act.
but there is one guy i can't delete
no matter how much silence there is.
he was like my big brother
growing up
and he died last year,
too fucking young.
i can't delete him.
death did that for me
and i just can't bring myself
to say goodbye in that
one
final way.

<u>enigma</u>

i am simultaneously
compassionate
and extremely judgmental.
these two things seem to co-exist
because certain things move me to
compassion,
and certain things
bug the living
hell out of me.
and the shit that bugs me
is usually stupid.
like if you fuck up the words
your and you're,
i'll totally jump in your shit.

bling

she wore jeans
with glitterballs on the pockets,
and carried a purse with a duck
on it.
expensive.
face done by mac.
nails in perfect squares
with blinding white tips
and a cap slung
sideways
to fool us
about her age.
she applies lipstick
manically while
she drives
and creates errands
that are unrelenting
so she never has to think about
how ordinary
she is on the
inside.

the rules

people are uniquely arbitrary
when choosing what rules
to follow.
i'm no exception.
for example,
even when no other cars are around,
i stop at stop signs
and signal when i turn.
i figure those rules are there
to keep me safe.
then there are the rules i break;
but
i figure those rules are there
to keep me mute.

power play

i went into a nude strip club alone
in portland.
i was doing research for a book.
despite the lithe,
twenty-something's completely nude
on stage,
i caught the interest of a guy
who sauntered over to me
and asked me if he could buy me
a drink.
i declined.
he looked at my notebook and asked me
what i was doing there.
i told him and then he asked the inevitable question:
what's your book about?
i told him it was about power.
he acted like he understood,
nodded,
began pontificating on how
men were using their power to
subjugate women,
especially there, in a place like that--
and i stopped him.
so you really think
you're the one with the power here?
both of our eyes turned to the stage
where a young woman
bent over slowly,
a smile on her face,
to gather up her pile of bills.

the heart

compassion
is at the heart
of everything good.
there are
no exceptions.

the stage

i've seen everything from high school,
to college,
to community,
to broadway.
i have yet to find a stage actor
who doesn't *act*
like a stage actor.
maybe
if they paid more attention
to the words
the playwright wrote
and less on their stage presence,
they would get it right.

will

your parents teach
and communicate
with more than words.
my dad had at least a couple mental illnesses
and probably some personality
disorders
and what my mother communicated to us
in a variety of ways
was that he just didn't put his shoulder into it;
he could help himself
with sheer force of will.
but he was too weak,
too selfish,
too feeble minded to do it.
my siblings and i
didn't get out unscathed.
we all self-flagellate
mercilessly about our weak wills,
when we should have been taught
mercy.

lights

we drove by a house
near my son's school
and i noted that there were
still lit pumpkin lights
on someone's porch.
it was the middle of february.
i almost made a snide remark
about halloween being over
but then i stopped;
what sort of thing
happens to a family
that makes a simple decoration
too hard to take down.
i shut my mouth
and felt a little sick inside.

dialogue

god: *i don't care if people are atheists;
as long as they're good people,
i'm happy.*
satan: *i don't care if people are religious;
as long as they're hypocritical and judgmental,
i'm happy.*

poetry slam

i watched a guy compete
in a poetry slam
and he faked having ocd
as part of his performance.
the end constituted him being *healed*
from his condition
because of
'true love'.
the audience,
true to form,
said
awwwwww.
i was caught in the mood too,
until i wasn't.
and then i was pissed.
because every ocd person
wishes love could cure them.
every depressed person feels guilty
that love can't cure them.
every bi-polar person tries
to make love cure them.
schizophrenics just want love
to make sense.
so fuck you,
mr. slam poet,
you simpering,
emotionally
manipulative dick.
fuck you for manipulating the pain of others
to win over your besotted audience—
fuck you for perpetuating the myth
that love—or anything
conquers all,
that mental illness is somehow linked to

the external
when in fact it's internal,
chemical,
and out of their control.
fuck you and your show.
if you're going to exploit people,
do it in a politically
incorrect way next time
so that people can actually see
what an asshole you are.

creation

no one was nice to her.
it was sixth grade but she was
already overweight
and had a nose like a pig,
all turned up,
freckled...
piggish.
i felt bad for her
because people were so mean to her
so i tried to be nice
even though
the danger was there;
the danger of getting social cooties
by not tormenting her.
but the strangest thing happened
when i was kind:
she was contemptuous of me,
mean,
unpleasant.
she made it really hard
to rise above it.
i didn't want to believe
that the bullying had already twisted her
into something hateful—
but maybe it did.
maybe it just doesn't take that long.

fixer-upper

we are a culture of victims.
we cultivate the wrongs done to us
like a fragile flower
in our windowsills.
b
   l
      a
         m
            e
slides out of us
at every turn of bad luck,
at every inevitable bad choice we make;
and we never deem ourselves responsible
because that would require a modicum of
self-awareness—
and why have self-awareness when there's
blame to be had.
then everything is out of our control.
then bad things happen
and we can get angry
and indignant
and demand that
the ubiquitous
they
fix it.
god forbid we should actually
do something proactive;
something that interrupts
our reality t.v.
and our latest
what-i-fucking-had-for-dinner
facebook update.

form

i wrote a villanelle,
a sestina,
a quatrain,
and a sonnet
just to prove i can.
now i write like this
so i can say whatever the fuck i want
without following
any
rules
at
all.

supportive

i was in a relationship
with a man
who had a curious reaction
to my small successes;
he seemed depressed by them,
as if they were a reflection
of all of his failures
echoing back into his past.
he would act underwhelmed,
then say with a sigh,
that's exciting.
he told me later
i would make it big someday
and i wouldn't need him.
i don't know that i buy
the idea that the whole time
he was worried about losing me.
had he been more excited
than i was at my victories,
maybe he wouldn't have.

taken

she was a photographer
with a broken camera.
a single mom,
trying to make her way
and so i proposed i lend her
the money
to buy a camera,
which led to a laptop,
which led to photoshop software
which led to her avoiding me for the
better part of a year.
when i finally called
we went to lunch.
in the car i told her to forget about the loan.
she didn't seem surprised
at my generosity.
she didn't even say
thank you;
instead she said,
okay,
like we'd come to some
mutual conclusion
together.
at lunch
the cashier rang us up
and she never even reached for
her wallet.
it was then
everything got
really, really clear.

flicks

i don't do chick-flicks.
i hate them, in fact.
i find them insulting
to every female
on the planet.
the spoken and unspoken message
of every fucking chick flick is:
you're better off with a man.
the storyline less cultivated
is that the chick in the movie
is a hot
sick mess
because of a man.
men are a lovely addition to our world;
but
they shouldn't
be
our world.

schoolyard

leave it to children
to pervert the literary devices of
alliteration and rhyme.
just ask any kid who has ever had
a derogatory nick-name.
no wonder kids hate poetry
from the get-go;
it was used in its very first form
to torment them.

bash

i don't get into male bashing
for male bashings' sake.
this whole culture has taken to it
because every other form of bashing
has been pc-ed out of existence.
the last population that is
allowed to be demeaned
is men.
we bitch when they're masculine,
we bitch when they're not strong,
we bitch when they're true to their natures,
we bitch when they don't instinctively
know ours.
they're in a no-win
and i think that's the way some women
like it.
it's bullshit.
make up your fucking minds
or leave them the fuck alone.

the heart 2

fear
is at the heart
of everything evil.
there are
no exceptions.

action

real love is a choice.
love is not something you stumble upon
or fall into
like an errant root
lifting up the soil
on a beaten path.
it's conscious,
it's deliberate,
and it's focused,
every day.
and this kind of love
is the only love that lasts.

support

there is a task no man has to suffer through
that women do every 1-2 years.
sure, the truly devoted man may suffer through it
second-hand,
but the actual experience is
a woman's alone.
bra shopping.
there is no amount of suck
that sucks enough
to describe the
suck
of how bad it sucks.

gut-punch

you try and explain
anxiety to people
who don't get anxiety,
and they immediately relate
by recalling a time
when they felt stressed about something.
about something.
anxiety is about
nothing.
nothing at all.
anxiety is the feeling
that someone just punched you
in the gut,
tore everything safe away,
and took all of the softness
out of the world.

big brother

i have a certain music playing program
on my computer.
every time i pull it up
it tells me it is not my default player;
would i like to make it my default player?
i invariably click
no.
then i'm afraid
because somehow,
somewhere,
i believe
they track that.
and i think
they   take   it   personally.

minx

the most dangerous type of woman
is the newly single woman.
she has her eyes out for anything with three legs.
anything.
but she's not out to snag a new one yet…
no.
what she's out for is
validation.
so she will look at you in that
come hither way;
her newly svelte form
from not eating
will sport scanty clothes,
she'll lead you on with her eyes,
her words,
her actions
until…..
she's got you.
whoever you are,
whatever you are.
and just when you think
you've got a shot with her,
she turns on an icy water stream.
her mission,
you poor gullible sap,
was to make sure
she's still got it.
you served your purpose by responding.
it's what they do.
just a head's up.

my public disagreement with eve ensler

i performed in eve ensler's
the vagina monologues.
all of the pieces are about vaginas
as you can imagine.
one piece, however, stands out
and it reeks
because it's disingenuous as hell.
it's called
my short skirt.
in this piece a woman,
wearing a very short skirt,
declares that her short skirt
is
not about you.
she opines that it's about empowerment,
who she is,
and to leave her the hell alone about it.
i mean, how dare you
get aroused by it, you pigs.
i say that every woman alive
who wears a short skirt
knows exactly what she's doing,
and to whom.
she wields her sexual power--
and to deny that she doesn't know
or care
about the effect it has on men
is bullshit.
she knows damn well.
if you're going to *own* your short skirt,
sweetheart,
it behooves you to at least be honest
with yourself
about why you're wearing it.

it sure as fuck isn't because
it's comfortable.

calling

it's tough to know why
people choose the professions they do.
i'm pretty sure i chose being a writer
and an artist
because in general,
people piss me off
and doing something solitary means
i don't have to deal
with all of their
fucking bullshit.
it's a theory.

breath mint

what is it
that makes
corn nuts so delicious
first hand
but so repulsive
second-hand
on someone's breath?

normal

there are times,
and they come quite often,
when i just want to be like
everyone else.
people argue with me.
no you don't, they say,
or
what is normal anyway?
they philosophize.
normal...
what is normal...
i'd say getting up and
working all day long at a job
is normal.
not having to take breaks
in a dark room,
heart pounding,
chest and gut in so much pain
you want to scream
is normal.
i say being able to go more than
one or two places
a day when you have five or six stops
to make is normal.
feeling like the world around you
is not your enemy,
having your productive time of day stop
when you decide,
not when the pain decides;
that is normal.
that's what i mean by normal.
so stop trying to make me feel better.
i want what you have,

i want what so many other people have.
i am sick
with jealousy about it.

disagreement

there's a new age wisdom
that's been batted about for years now:
don't take anything personally.
i call bullshit on that.
this is just another way you get to say to yourself
i'm okay just as i am
and it's their problem.
but sometimes it isn't.
sometimes it's your fucking problem
and you should absolutely
take it fucking personally.
you might learn something
about yourself.

the teacher

they say that history is
our greatest teacher,
but i think we mustn't discount
the power of stories.
there is a common theme
in most folk tales that gets completely ignored
but always remains true to form:
the sin of hubris.
it's what i think about
with every bumper sticker i see
proclaiming america the best country,
america, the most powerful country,
america and its divine right.
i always think of the stories,
the arrogance,
the fall of the once mighty.
it makes me want to tell people
a story.
it makes me want to reanimate
the disgraced dead
and see them cluck their tongues at us
and shake their heads in knowing
apprehension.

stepping out

adultery is never the reason
for a divorce.
content
satiated men
do not cheat.
content
fulfilled women
do not cheat.
it's the thousand little steps
created or missed,
the things taken
for granted,
the communication
never rising above the mundane
and ordinary,
the effort unmade to
look,
feel,
think,
grow…
a thousand little steps
not toward one another,
but away—
that's what causes
cheating.
adultery
is simply the reason
one of you
gets to pretend you're the victim.

settle

there were nights
when i would go to bars
hell-bent on getting laid.
it was never ideal,
and never who i really wanted,
but i never had the heart to say
well, you'll just have to do.

the torture

when she lost her lover
the torture didn't just come just from
the loss,
but from the knowledge
that her former lover
never even thinks of her
at all.

visitor

she reminds me
of a big, vanilla
balloon...
so pale
shapeless
never uttering a word
even when we say
hello
and
come join the group.
her timid face turns away
and she takes a chair in the very back,
never saying a word
never reading a word-
she listens to our poetry
and her only reaction
is a flushed face
and eyes cast down
to look at her swollen fingers.
but she is there, at a poetry group;
she has a folder filled with paper.
i wonder what sort of agony
keeps her silent.
i wonder
what sort of fear
haunts her
into an oblivious stare
as we break for the night
and she hurries off
without ever meeting a gaze.

ascension

being pulled up the stairs
by your hair
is
not
just another way to say
i love you.

double trouble

i glanced at the woman in the
newspaper.
blond, slim, librarian glasses...
she was
h-o-t.
and she was in hot water.
she's an english teacher and
it seems she's being accused
of statutory rape of one of her
male students.
i mean stat rape is stat rape right?
but
just ask any grown man...
they'll tell you.
every one of them
envies the shit
outta that kid.

ultimatum

i was looking at him
in the bathroom mirror
as he stood in the doorway.
i told him that
if he ever touched me in anger again
i'd leave.
i'd leave for good.
his reaction spilt me in two.
he said,
i can't promise you that—
and i can't live with that
kind of pressure!
there was no going back, then
and i told him so.
then he did something so
unexpected;
he went down the hall,
weeping aloud
and went into our
four year-old daughter's room.
he picked her up out of her bed
when she was fast asleep
and soon she was crying
out of fear and confusion…
he sobbed in her hair and said
mommy is breaking up
our happy family!
it was then i knew
i was dealing
with a psychopath.

let it go

buddhism
is just existential angst
with an optimistic twist.

plump

we sat at a table at mcdonald's—
it was my boyfriend, his best friend and i.
they were talking about one of my best friends,
becky.
it was the 80's and becky had been blessed
with the ideal 80's body—
big tits
and straight-as-a-boy hips,
no ass
down below.
they were clearly impressed
with becky.
i was not meant for the 80's.
i had a small waist,
curvy hips
and a very round,
prominent ass.
i started getting a little miffed
and said
what, so i'm a fatty?
my boyfriend looked at me
with a bemused expression and said
no, you're not fat....
you're....
pleasant.

i've never stopped
seeing myself
through that deceptively
misnamed
lens.

hot

jaeger has an interesting
effect on me.
it raises my body temperature
so much so
that i feel i need to disrobe
when i drink it.
when people offer it to me,
just to save time
i tell them
i don't drink jaeger,
it makes my clothes fall off.
this never seems to have the desired effect--
they order it for me anyway.

the game

shooting straight doesn't work.
straight shooters,
honest people,
they are honest for themselves,
not for others.
the manipulative game players
will always win,
always come out on top
because it's always about getting ahead
and they will do whatever it takes.
and unless you're willing to betray yourself
you are left with only your principals
to keep you warm.
people are far more interested
in a fairy tale
than in truth.

a decision

i want to know
how to get my faith back.
i want to believe in something again.
it was such a point of comfort
and i didn't see how the loss of it
would affect everything.
i looked at my mother's picture today
and i spoke to her;
i told her that if i could just believe
that when i die
it would be like a homecoming
and she and dad would be there

then i could deal with her being gone.
i could deal with a lot of stuff,
actually.
if i could only believe.
my words seemed to pour out of me,
hit the wall
and come back,
an echo of loss,
a reverberation
of futility.
i know it's just a decision,
i told her,
making a choice to believe.
but i made the choice
to stop self-deception
a long time ago
as a matter of principle.
she answered me with her smile
and her unblinking eyes.
and i felt silly for a second,
talking to myself like that.
i felt silly,
and then i started to cry.

escape

there's no escaping it.
everybody has a
goofy uncle.

acquaintance

she was eighteen when she started
to go to the parties.
any one she could find,
anywhere.
frat houses were her favorite.
she did a beer bong
and chugged four beers
and did shots of tequila
and some shot with
orange fizz soda and then her friend
who had been working the room
would hook up with someone
if she didn't first.
and so one night
at a house party
she found a bed
and was nearly passed out
when this guy came in
and got on top of her.
it's so hard to say no when
you're almost passed out
and your skirt is that short
and you can't push hard.
something inside gives up
until you're stone sober
in the morning,
which she was
when she finally called
rape.
she told people
and told her ex-boyfriend
and he asked her if she had
called the police.
no,

*she said,
i can't.
i knew him—
we went out
a couple of times.*

kokomo club

the couple in the corner just got
engaged last week.
he took her to his favorite hangout
and they played pool
then he pulled her into
the dingy men's room
and fucked her up against the sink.
she wasn't the first girl he'd brought
in there.

so dark

there was a night so dark.
i was alone,
my daughters at their father's
for a whole week.
that was the arrangement.
one week with him,
one week with me;
no fighting it.
he had parents with money
and i had none.
the war inside me began
as a slow burn.
i was split in two--
had a whole bottle of pills
spread out
on the floor in front of me
as i sat there,
sobbing.
i pulled out the pictures my daughters drew,
pictures of them,
with me, the kitty, sunshine;
the cards they made
for mother's day
covered in flowers--
i placed them before me on the floor.
one by one,
i picked up each pill
and placed them on top
of every carefully drawn line,
each bright colored crayoned bloom
until i couldn't see the pills
without gazing directly
at what i would leave
behind.

two-fer

the night before
we went out as friends.
we'd always been friends
and then alcohol made us
grope in the parking lot
and fuck in my bed.
he went all fucking night
and i thought my cunt would
fuse to his cock
and get ripped out with every thrust
he gave me from behind.
he kept saying he had been waiting to do
it with me
for so long.
i wanted—no—needed
him to finish and leave.
i had another guy coming over
to take me to brunch
and i needed to replenish my fluids
before i fucked him on
the couch.

for the win

someone once sneered
that i was a trophy wife.
i wish i had been there;
i would have thanked them.
trophy wives
are hot.

article 13

i believe in being honest,
direct, lascivious, compassionate,
opinionated
and in telling it like it is
to all men (and women);
indeed i may say that i follow
the admonition of christopher hitchens—
i believe what can be proved,
i am dubious even then,
i've been through a lot of shit,
and i won't put up with
your shit.
if there is anything artistic, substantial,
authentic,
realistic, or fucking glorious,
with a fiery vengeance, i seek after these things.[1]

---

1 Article 13 of the Mormon Articles of Faith: "We believe in being honest, true, chaste, benevolent, virtuous, and in doing good to all men; indeed, we may say that we follow the admonition of Paul- We believe all things, we hope all things, we have endured many things, and hope to be able to endure all things. If there is anything virtuous, lovely, or of good report or praiseworthy, we seek after these things."

imperfect

i am so grateful
my parents were flawed.
they were as devout a mormon
as flawed people could be—
and this paved the way for them
to be accepting
of their heathen daughter
at my very worst.
when they got older
it was me,
the heathen daughter,
who took care of them.
then they saw the rest;
they saw me at my very best.

∽∾

e y z f c

so i took my son to the eye doctor.
the doctor was making notes in his computer and
i started to wonder
if his wife ever gave him head.
then i wondered what was wrong with me.

infinite

the capacity for love
in the human heart is infinite;
where we make the mistake is
assuming everyone
takes it to its potential.

release

there is something
so cathartic about writing a poem
fueled by pent-up emotions—
emotions so strong that they could
eat a hole through you
if you don't get them out,
on paper,
for you and the world to see.

<u>try</u>

my first husband
had some artistic ability.
one day he brought out
some oil paints and a small canvas
and told me to have a go
at painting.
so i did.
i had never painted before,
never taken an art class
but i did my rendition of a ship
on the ocean
and i remember feeling some pride
when i finished.
when my husband saw it,
he laughed at it—out loud.
then he patted my head and said
aww, you tried, didn't you?
it took me fifteen years
to pick up a paint brush to paint.
now,
over thirty pieces of my art
rest in galleries
all over the city.
in other words,
i tried again.

moments

i don't think i'll ever look
at moments
the same way.
i found out
this kid i went to high school with—
a kid i worked with at a pizzeria,
died recently.
i only had one real memory of him.
he was a good mormon boy,
hung out with the mormon
aristocracy in our school,
and one night
while taking out the garbage at work
he grabbed me
and kissed me
and shoved his hand
up my shirt.
that moment
is how i remember him.
i don't think
that's how he would have wanted
to be remembered.
i'm not angry.
i learned that for better or for worse
every moment we have counts.
it's what he taught me in life
and through his death;
so be careful with your moments.
r.i.p. kevin.

signs

did i know you are a scorpio?
no, i didn't.
i would have guessed your sign to be
'monumentally gullible
and unreasonably stupid.'

maturity

one sunday i sat in a café
and watched a mother
eat brunch with her kids;
the grandmother was there, too
and the grandmother started
shaming
the youngest boy
because he hadn't combed his hair.
she was relentless,
going on and on
at him…
i wondered how she could have
lived this long
and not learned anything.

rugrats

i have a complex relationship
with children.
not my own, of course;
that's easy.
it's all the other smelly,
loud,
obnoxious,
ill-mannered,
smelly--did i say smelly?
spawn of
everyone else.
like i said:
complex.

chimes

this guy told me about the time
he want on a nude cruise.
there was this woman walking around
with what basically amounted to
wind chimes
dangling from her cunt.
tinkle tinkle tinkle...
it made me wonder
what sort of impending storm
she was actually expecting.

ba-da-bang

mormon church doctrine
teaches that god came down and
impregnated mary
in the manner of the flesh.
so—flesh and blood god,
fucking a fourteen year old
betrothed to someone else.
i'm extremely curious
about how that went down,
exactly.

journey

they say
life is a journey—
that may be true, but…
i'm consistently surprised
at how light
some people pack.

fugitives

we have a coffee shop that's ours.
we go there a couple of times a month
for sunday brunch
to eat, write, talk...
the shop is owned by a mother and daughter.
when the daughter was four years old
she had to go into hiding
with her mother
because her father
was after them,
trying to kill them.
i can't imagine the strength
of this woman
and the resiliency of her daughter
to go through something like that.
they live here, now,
in this little corner
of the world, smiling,
talking, serving coffee...
i wonder sometimes
as i watch them,
if they finally feel completely safe--
or
if they ever will.

vagina mine

there were once these two mormon
guys
famous in 'these here parts'.
during the 1920's all the way through the '40's
they had a vicious,
personal vendetta
against each other—
public disputes that were
well-known and well-documented.
i personally fucked
both of their great-grandsons.
i like to think that
if there is a heaven,
they are friends now,
brought together
by the peace-pipe of my cunt.

∽∾

the engineer

we were at my art gallery opening.
we began talking to
someone—
the gentleman was 94 and a ww2 vet.
he had also been an engineer,
and he regaled us
with story after story
after story
of his adventures,
all the while
staring directly
at my tits.
i was actually sort of impressed.

my piece

i have moments where
regret tears at me
until i can't rest.
those moments are invariably
when i don't speak up,
say my piece,
to the faces of people
who deserve to be told
that whatever just spewed
out of their mouths
was
offensive and obscene.
in other words
i chickened out
to keep the peace.
but i kept the peace
at the expense of my own.

simple

i watched the car ahead of me
at a stop light.
the black labrador's head stuck out
of the back window,
the sun gleaming on his snout.
he sniffed the air,
took in everything around him--
the light changed
and the car started moving
and right away
the dog's tail
began wagging
and wagging
and what if
it was just that simple?

resolved

*motherfucking
muppet-fuckers.*

JA Carter-Winward lives and writes in the mountains of northern Utah.

Always Listen to the Ravings of a Mad Woman (under Henneman)

TDTM

Falling Back to Earth

The Rub: A Novel

Grind: A Novel

No Apologies

Shorts: A Collection (short stories)

CPSIA information can be obtained
at www.ICGtesting.com
Printed in the USA
LVOW04s0253040316
477751LV00019B/745/P